CTS Primary
Religious Education

3

Pupil Book

Anne-Marie Allison

CATHOLIC TRUTH SOCIETY
PUBLISHERS TO THE HOLY SEE

Introduction

Welcome to *'The Way, the Truth & the Life'* series. Think about the name of this series of books.

It is Jesus who said: "I am the Way, the Truth and the Life". So it is Jesus who shows us the **Way** to lead a good and happy life, he tells us the **Truth** about God and he gives us new **Life** in the sacraments.

As you progress through your lessons in religious education this year, you will learn about the Sacrament of Baptism, the Sacrament of Reconciliation and the Sacrament of the Eucharist. Also, you will learn more about the life of Jesus and what it means to be a Christian, one of his close friends.

Most of all you will come to see how important our faith is, and how much it helps us as we grow up.

I hope that you will spend time everyday with Jesus in prayer.

+Vincent Nichols

✠ Vincent Nichols
Archbishop of Birmingham

Contents

1. The Christian Family

A gift from God

Think about what it means to be part of a family

When Jesus was a little boy he lived with his parents, Mary and Joseph, in their house in Nazareth. Jesus loved his family very much and Mary and Joseph took very good care of him.

Jesus, Mary and Joseph did lots of things together. They played together, they ate their meals together, they prayed together and they helped each other with all the jobs that had to be done. They shared many happy times as a family, and some sad times too.

We all belong to a family! Some of us belong to a big one, and others a small one.

Your family is a gift to you from God. God gave you a family so that you would have people to take care of you and to love you. You do special things just like Jesus did and you can probably think of lots of happy times you have shared together.

Being part of a family is not always easy. We all have times when we find it difficult. There may be times when our parents don't agree with each other. Sometimes we argue with brothers or sisters. Occasionally, we leave all the jobs to one person, or get fed up of having to share all the time. No family is perfect!

 # Activities

1. Make a list of some of the things you enjoy doing with your family, for example watching TV or going for a walk.

2. Choose one very special time that you and your family have enjoyed together and write about it.

3. Here are some of the problems that can arise in family life. Read each one in turn and write down a possible solution to the problem.

At the end of the day, Mario's family relax in different ways: he goes out on his bike, his big sister watches television and Dad reads the newspaper, but Mum always seems to be in the kitchen washing and tidying up after supper. Can you think of a solution?

Every Saturday night, Jo's family sit down together for a family dinner. This means that Jo always misses her favourite programme on television. Jo wants to watch her programme and have her dinner later but her Mum says she has to sit down and eat with everyone else. Can you think of a solution?

Francesca and Marco always argue about whose turn it is on the computer. Everyone else in their family is fed up of listening to them quarrel. Can you think of a solution?

4. What do you do to help in your family?

The Christian family

Think about what it means to be part of the Christian family

As well as our own family, we belong to the Christian family. This is made up of people just like us.

Christians are people who know from Jesus that God loves them very much. They want to learn to love as Jesus did. Our Christian family is very big and we have brothers and sisters all over the world in every country. We call this big family the **Church**.

Our Christian family is so big that we cannot all meet together in the same place! Instead we meet as a much smaller group in our **parish** family, led by our **parish priest**.

A parish is all the people in our Christian family who live near each other.

We meet with our parish family each week when we go to Mass and at special times throughout the year, such as Easter and Christmas.

Our **parish church** is a special building where all the people who live in our parish can come together so that we can praise and thank God as part of his family.

 **Activities**

1. Match each word or phrase below with its correct meaning.

The Christian family	A special building where we meet with our Christian family to praise God
Parish	He leads our parish family
Parish priest	People who love God and want to live like Jesus
Parish church	All the people in our Christian family who live near each other

2. Can you think of a time when you have met with your parish family at a Mass for a special occasion?

   (a) Write about this time.

   (b) Make a list of some of the things that happen when the Christian family meets together at Mass.

Research

3. **My Parish Family**

   (a) Find out the name of your parish church and your parish priest.

   (b) Make a list of some of the people and groups who work in your parish family.

   (c) Choose **one** of these and find out as much as you can about the work that they do.

   (d) Imagine you will have the opportunity to interview a parish priest about his work and his parish. Working in pairs, write a list of questions that you would like to ask him.

> ### Word Box
> parish   church
> Mass   celebrate
> Parish Church   parish priest

Joining the Christian family

Know that we join the Christian family when we are baptised

When did we become part of our Christian family, the Church? We joined the Church when we were **baptised**. For most of us this was when we were little babies.

Our parents wanted us to be baptised because they wanted us to grow up in the love of God, to be part of his Christian family and to live our lives as Jesus showed us.

On the day that we were baptised, the priest called us by our own name. This is our **Christian name** because when we were baptised we became Christians, followers of Jesus Christ and we joined the Christian family.

Being a Christian means we should try to live our lives in a Christian way, just as Jesus taught us to when he was on earth.

He was loving and kind to everyone he met, even to his enemies, and he was always willing to forgive people when they did something wrong.

As baptised Christians we should try to be like Jesus and show love and kindness to all the people we meet, even to those who are unkind to us.

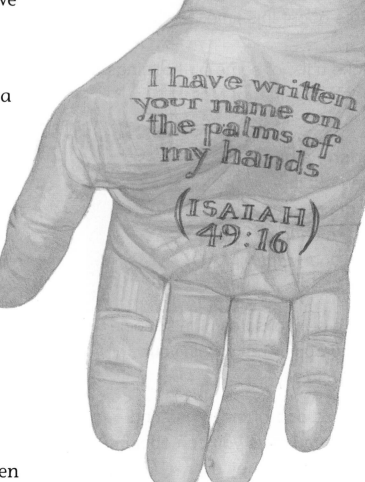

I have written your name on the palms of my hands

(ISAIAH 49:16)

 Activities

1. Think about the words from the prophet Isaiah: "I have written your name on the palms of my hands." What do you think God is saying to us here?

2. Listen to or read the story from the Gospel of Mark about Jesus healing the paralysed man. (Mk 2:1-12)

   (a) Imagine you have the chance to interview the paralysed man after Jesus has healed him.

   (b) What questions would you like to ask him? Write them down.

   (c) Now write down what he might have said in response to each question.

3. Our Christian family is made up of people who want to live like Jesus lived. What do you think 'living like Jesus' means?

4. (a) Write down the names of three people you will meet today.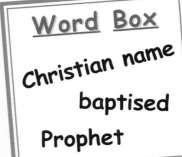

   (b) Next to each name write down some ways you could show kindness to them.

5. (a) Make a list of all the words in the word box opposite.

   (b) Look them up in the glossary and write down their meanings.

   (c) Learn the meanings of the words by heart.

Word Box

Christian name

baptised

Prophet

Your Baptism

On the day that you joined the Christian family, your parents took you to Church to be baptised either during Mass or during a special baptism service.

Know what happens when we are baptised

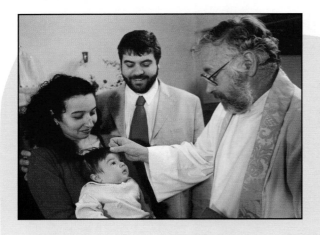

The priest welcomed your family and made the **sign of the cross** on your forehead.

You were baptised at a special place in the church called the **baptismal font**. Here you were blessed or **anointed** with oil.

Your parents and **godparents** made **baptismal promises** and said they would bring you up as a **child of God**.

Water that had been blessed was poured over your head three times as the priest said "I baptise you in the name of the Father and of the Son and of the Holy Spirit."

After this you were anointed again with another oil. A **white garment** was wrapped around you and you were given a **baptismal candle**.

Finally, everyone joined in as your family said the prayer Jesus taught us, the **Our Father**. From then on, you became a Christian and a member of the Christian family, the Church.

Activities

1. Draw five simple pictures of different things that happen during a baptism and underneath each picture write a sentence explaining what is happening.

2. Find out as much as you can about your own baptism and record your research on the baptism record sheet that your teacher will give you.

3. Find out why your name was chosen for you.

My Name is...

4. Make a list of all the words in the Word Box.

   (a) Look up the meaning of the words in the Glossary and write them down.

   (b) Learn the meaning of the words by heart.

Word Box

baptismal garment

baptismal promises

baptismal font

godparents

anointed

baptismal water

baptismal candle

Signs used in Baptism

If you look around your classroom or your school you can probably find lots of different signs.

Each sign tells you something; for example, a fire exit sign tells you where to leave the room if there is a fire. Signs are used in baptism as well. Just like the signs in your school, the signs used in baptism tell you important things!

You can find out more about the signs used in baptism below and why they are used.

Water
Water is a sign of life - without it we could not live! When water is poured over the baby in baptism it is a sign that the baby is sharing in the new life of Jesus.

Sign of the Cross
The Sign of the Cross is an important sign for Christians because Jesus died on the cross and rose again after three days.

The Sign of the Cross is made on the child's forehead to show that the baby is now part of the Christian family.

Candle
Jesus is the Light of the World and the baptismal candle is a sign that the light of Christ has entered the baby's life. This candle is lit from the Easter or **Paschal candle** which usually has its own place in the church.

White Garment

This is usually a white shawl or dress and is wrapped around the baby towards the end of the baptism. The shawl is put on the baby as a sign that the baby has 'put on' Christ and shares in the new life of Jesus.

Oil

A special oil that has been blessed by the bishop is poured on the baby's head as a sign of the presence of the Holy Spirit who will help the baby in his or her Christian life.

 # Activities

1. **(a)** Draw some of the signs you see every day in school or on the way to school.

   (b) What does each sign tell you?

2. Copy and complete this chart:

3. Imagine someone you know is going to have their baby baptised soon. Design and make a baptism card, decorated with suitable symbols, that you could give them on their special day.

4. Write a prayer to thank God for the day you received the Sacrament of Baptism. Include in your prayer all the people you think were present that day.

Sign used in baptism	What that sign tells me
Candle	Jesus is the light of the world.

Word Box

Paschal candle   bishop

Holy Spirit

13

Promises made at Baptism

A Broken Promise?

It was Sita's birthday and she was having a big party with lots of friends coming over to her house. She had been looking forward to it for ages, especially when she heard that her best friend Jenny was coming too! Jenny used to go to the same school, but then Jenny's family had moved out of the area. Now they didn't see each other very much.

Jenny had rung Sita during the week.
"Yes of course I'm coming," she had said.
"I promise! I can't wait to see you again!"

But now it was the day of the party and everyone was there except for Jenny. Sita knew she should be joining in the fun and enjoying herself, but it just wasn't the same without Jenny. She felt so disappointed - how could Jenny have broken her promise?

Suddenly the phone rang and when Sita lifted up the receiver she was delighted to hear Jenny's voice on the other end. "Oh Sita, I'm so sorry. Mum's car broke down. But don't worry, a taxi is on its way and we should be with you in an hour." "I thought you weren't going to come," said Sita with relief. "Don't be silly," replied her friend. "I promised I'd be there, didn't I?"

We all know how important promises are, and how important it is to keep a promise made to a friend. Promises are very important in the **Sacrament** of Baptism.

On the day that you were baptised your parents and godparents made very special promises before God. They promised that they believed in God, our Father, in Jesus Christ his Son and in the Holy Spirit. They promised to bring you up as a Christian and they promised to be a good example to you of how a Christian should live.

Your parents chose two or more people to be your godparents. Your godparents were probably very good friends of your parents or even members of your family. They had to choose your godparents very carefully because they needed good people to help them in their task of bringing you up as a member of God's Christian family.

 ## Activities

1. **(a)** How did Sita feel when Jenny promised to come to her party?

   (b) How did she feel when she thought Jenny had broken her promise?

   (c) Can you think of an important promise that someone made to you?

   (d) Did they keep their promise? How did this make you feel?

   (e) Why do you think a promise made should be kept and not broken?

2. Imagine you are a parent choosing a godparent for your child.

   (a) What sort of person are you looking for?

   (b) What important qualities should she or he have?

 ## Research

3. Find out the names of your godparents.

   (a) Ask your parents why they chose them.

   (b) If possible, talk to your godparents and find out about their memories of your special day. How did they feel about being chosen as your godparents?

Baptism is a Sacrament

Our Baptism is a very special moment. It marks
the beginning of our Christian journey through life.
Baptism is such a special event that the Church calls it a **sacrament**.
There are seven sacraments in the Church and they mark
all the important moments in our Christian life.

When we were baptised, we received the
first of the seven sacraments.
As we journey through life we
will receive others, such as the
Sacrament of the **Eucharist**
or maybe the Sacrament of
Marriage. Each sacrament
will bring us closer to God
and makes us stronger
followers of Jesus.

In every sacrament we receive, God
offers us a very special gift or grace to help
us on our journey; for example, in Baptism the
grace offered to us by God is to be part of the Christian
family, the Church.

 ## Activities

1. On a card draw a picture of what you think your Baptism was like.
   Remember to put in all the important things about it.

2. On the other side of the card write the story of your Baptism and explain why it
   was so important.

3. How do you think the Sacrament of Baptism will help you as you get older?

Rite of Baptism

Priest: What name do you give your child?

Parents: John

Priest: What do you ask of God's Church for John?

Parents: Baptism.

The priest addresses the parents in these or similar words:

You have asked to have your child baptised. In doing so you are accepting the responsibility of training him in the practice of the faith. It will be your duty to bring him up to keep God's commandments as Christ taught us, by loving God and our neighbour. Do you clearly understand what you are undertaking?

Parents: We do.

Then the priest turns to the godparents: Are you ready to help the parents of this child in their duty as Christian parents?

Godparents: We are.

Priest: John, the Christian community welcomes you with great joy. In its name I claim you for Christ our Saviour by the sign of his cross. I now trace the cross on your forehead, and invite your parents and godparents to do the same.

4. Read the **Rite of Baptism** text and then answer the questions below.

(a) What do you think is the most important thing that the priest is saying to the parents?

(b) What do the godparents have to do?

Word Box
Eucharist   saviour   Marriage
commandments   grace
Rite of Baptism   sacrament

2. Mary Our Mother

God calls Mary

Has anyone ever asked you to do a really important job? Perhaps you have a pet of

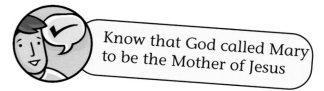

Know that God called Mary to be the Mother of Jesus

your own that you have to look after, or maybe you've been asked to care for a younger brother or sister for a short while.

Ben was excited. Today, Mrs Barnes the Headteacher, was going to introduce him to the new boy, Francesco, who was joining his class today. Francesco came from Italy. Ben knew he had to look after him for a whole week.

"This is Francesco. Promise me you'll take good care of him," said Mrs Barnes. "Don't forget to show him where everything is." "I promise," said Ben, and Francesco tried to smile, even if he looked a bit lost.

All week Ben worked hard and kept his promise to Mrs Barnes. He got to school a bit early to show Francesco where the school hall and sports room were.

He went with him into the playground and they played with his best friends, Daniel and Mike.

When school finished he stayed with him until his Mum came to pick him up. By the end of the week, Ben and Francesco had become great friends.

On Friday, Mrs Barnes came to see how things were, and was delighted to see Francesco looking so well and happy. "Thank you Ben," she said. "You've really taken great care of him. Next time I need someone to do an important job, I'll know who to ask!"

In the Bible we can read about a time when God chose someone really special to do a very important job for Him. God wanted someone to be the mother of his son, Jesus, someone who was kind and good and who would love his son very much.

The Annunciation, by Edward Frampton

One day, God sent the Angel Gabriel to see a young girl called Mary who lived in Nazareth. Mary loved God very much so she listened carefully to what the Angel Gabriel had to say.

The Annunciation, by Rossetti

"Hail Mary!" said the angel. "The Lord is with you."

Mary was very surprised to be spoken to in this way but the angel said-

"Do not be afraid Mary for I bring you good news."

The angel explained to Mary that God had chosen her to be the mother of a baby boy and that the baby would be called Jesus.

He told Mary that this baby would be very special and holy because he would be God's son.

Mary was amazed to hear all this, but she knew that God loved her and she wanted to do whatever he asked of her.

She told the angel that she would be the Mother of Jesus and then the angel left.

God chose someone to do an important job for him.

Although Mary was just an ordinary young girl in lots of ways, God knew that she loved him very much and that she would love and care for Jesus.

The Annunciation, by Fra Angelico

 ## Activities

1. **(a)** What job was Ben given to do in the story?

   (b) Did he do this job well?

   (c) Why do you think Mrs Barnes chose Ben for this job?

2. Think about some of the jobs you have been asked to do during this past week, then copy out and complete the chart below.

Jobs I have been given	Why I was chosen for the job	How well I did the job

3. Copy this story into your book and fill in the missing words; the box below will help you.

The Angel Gabriel appeared to _____.

Mary felt _____.

The Angel said 'The _____ be with you.

Blessed are you among all _____.

God has chosen you to be the _____ of his son.

He will be called _____.

Mary bowed her head and said _____.

Then the Angel _____.

afraid

vanished

appeared

Yes

Jesus

gone

Mary

lonely

Lord

women

mother

4. **(a)** What job did God choose Mary to do?

(b) Why do you think God chose Mary for this job?

(c) Do you think Mary did this job well? Why?

5. Look at the paintings of the Annunciation on pages 19 and 20.

(a) Which do you think illustrates the story best. Explain Why?

Word Box

Annunciation   Angel Gabriel

Mary says 'Yes' to God

Know how Mary answered God's call

Sometimes people ask us to do jobs that we really want to do, just like Ben really wanted to look after Francesco in the story. When this happens, it's easy to say 'yes' and to do the job well. But sometimes people ask us to do things that we don't really want to do and then it becomes much harder to smile and agree to do the job.

Mary was a young girl when God asked her to be the Mother of Jesus. She probably felt very frightened at the thought of being a mother and she may have had other plans for her life. Mary had a choice - she did not have to do what God asked of her. She could have been selfish and said 'No' to God.

But Mary loved God very much and she knew that he loved her. She did not know what the future had in store for her, but her faith in God was very great. She put her trust in God and said 'Yes' to him.

Just as God called Mary, so he calls each one of us. Every day God asks us to be good Christians, to show love to our friends and family and to be kind and thoughtful. Just like Mary, we have a choice. We can say 'Yes' to God and do what he asks of us, or we can be selfish and say 'No' to God.

When we pray, we can ask Jesus and Mary to help us to be kind and loving so that we always do what God wants us to do.

Activities

1. Write about a time when someone asked you to do a job that you did not want to do.

   (a) How did you react?

   (b) What happened?

   (c) How did you feel afterwards?

2. **(a)** Do you think Mary wanted to do the job that God asked her to do?

   (b) How did she respond?

3. God calls us to be good Christians. Draw or write about one way we can show love and kindness to:

   (a) someone in our class;

   (b) someone in our family;

   (c) someone who is lonely.

4. **(a)** Can you think of a time when you or someone else found it hard to say 'Yes' to God?

   (b) Draw or write about this time.

   (c) Write a 'sorry' prayer and place it in your prayer corner.

Research

5. Look in a book of Bible stories or a book of saints and find out about some men and women who, like Mary, said 'yes' to God. Prepare a presentation for your class.

Mary our Mother

Think about how Mary shows her love for us, and how we can show our love for her

Mary plays an important role in our lives. Because she is the Mother of Jesus, she is our mother too. She is our mother in heaven and she loves us as her very own children. From her home in heaven she shows her love for us by watching over us and listening to our prayers.

There are many ways that the Church remembers Mary during the year and honours her as the Mother of Jesus.

We sing hymns and carols about Mary, and how God chose her to be the mother of his son.

We have statues of her in our homes or schools or church to remind us that she said 'Yes' to God.

We go to Mass on her great feast days to thank her for her kindness and love.

We pray to Mary using our own words or we can say Mary's very special prayer, the **Hail Mary**.

The Hail Mary is based on the words of the Angel Gabriel, and the words of Mary's cousin Elizabeth when Mary went to visit her.

Hail Mary, full of grace,
the Lord is with thee.
Blessed art thou among women
and blessed is the fruit
of thy womb,
Jesus.

Holy Mary, Mother of God,
pray for us sinners,
now and at the
hour of our death.
Amen.

Soon after the angel's visit, Mary went to see her cousin Elizabeth who lived with her husband Zechariah.

Mary greeted Elizabeth, and Elizabeth knew through the Holy Spirit that Mary was going to have a baby, a very important baby, the son of God. She said, "Mary, you are the most holy of all women and the child you will have is most holy! How is it that the woman who is going to have God's son should come and visit me?"

Mary spoke words of praise and love for God. She stayed with Elizabeth for three months and then she went home to Nazareth.

We remember Elizabeth's words to Mary every time we say the Hail Mary -
*'Blessed art thou among women
and blessed is the fruit of thy womb, Jesus'.*

These words remind us that Mary was *'blessed'* - that means chosen and holy - and that the child she gave birth to was the Son of God, who would grow up to become the saviour of the world.

Activities

1. **(a)** Use a hymn book to help you find some hymns about Mary.

   (b) Select your favourite verse or phrase. Why did you choose this one?

   (c) Write your own song or hymn to Mary.

2. **(a)** Look at the different images of Mary on page 24.

   Which is your favourite? Why?

   (b) Design your own image of Mary using the pictures on page 24 to help you.

3. **(a)** Work with a partner and together re-write the Hail Mary in words that we would use and understand today.

   (b) Choose one sentence from the Hail Mary and, with your partner, illustrate these words for display.

4. Imagine you are Mary writing a letter to your cousin Elizabeth.

   Dear Elizabeth,

   Just writing a note to tell you....

   love from...

   (a) Tell her all about the visit from the angel and the good news he gave you.

   (b) Tell her how you felt when you heard what the angel had to say and what answer you gave.

Word Box

statue

feast

Hail Mary

saviour

The Visitation, by Philippe de Champaigne

5. Look at the painting of 'The Visitation' above.

   (a) Why is this event called 'The Visitation'?

   (b) Explain briefly what is happening in the picture.

   (c) How can you tell who is Elizabeth and who is Mary?

   (d) How would you describe the expressions on their faces?

The Hail Mary

6. (a) Read the Hail Mary on page 25.

   (b) Write down the part of this prayer that Elizabeth said to Mary.

   (c) Learn to say the whole prayer by heart.

We prepare to celebrate the birth of Jesus

The four weeks leading up to Christmas are an important time for Christians. We call this time Advent. During Advent we prepare to celebrate the birth of Jesus. The word Advent means 'coming' and during Advent we think especially about the coming of Jesus at Christmas.

This can be a very exciting time as we rush around wrapping Christmas presents, writing Christmas cards, decorating trees. But it is very important that we remember what we are really preparing for - the birth of Jesus.

There are lots of ways we can remind ourselves during Advent of the great event that will happen on Christmas Day.

Advent Wreath

The Advent wreath has four candles, one for each week of Advent. Some wreaths have a fifth white candle in the middle to be lit on Christmas Day. By lighting the candles on the Advent wreath and saying Advent prayers, we remember that we are waiting for Jesus to come at Christmas.

Crib

Every church and lots of homes have cribs during Advent. When we look at a crib we remember where and how Jesus was born.

Christmas Cards

Sending Christmas cards is a lovely way to remind people that we are waiting for Jesus to be born. Have a good look at the Christmas cards you receive this year (look at these ones here) and sort them into two piles - ones that show that we are waiting for the coming of Jesus, and ones which don't.

Advent Promise

Another way we can prepare for the coming of the Son of God is to make an Advent promise. This can be something very simple, like setting aside a little time every day to talk and pray to Jesus, or promising to be extra helpful at home. You don't have to tell anyone your promise - it is between you and God.

Activities

1. Make an Advent promise! Spend some time thinking about what this might be then write it down on a holly leaf shape and place it in your class prayer corner.

2. Design a Christmas card that you could send to a friend. Make sure your card shows what Christmas is really about.

3. Write a letter to Jesus. Tell him why you are looking forward to his birthday and ask for something that would bring happiness to others.

Research

4. Find out about Christmas customs in different countries.

God becomes man

As we prepare during Advent to celebrate the coming of God among us this Christmas, we can remember how Mary our Mother prepared for this same event over 2000 years ago!

Not long before Jesus was born, Mary and Joseph had to make another journey. This time they had a very long way to go, all the way to Bethlehem!

This would have been a long journey in those days when there were no trains or buses or cars! When Mary and Joseph arrived in Bethlehem the town was so busy that there was no room in any of the inns and nowhere for them to stay.

Mary must have felt very tired and weary by this time. When they were offered a stable for the night, she was delighted.

These days when a woman is having a baby there is a long list of things that have to be bought - a cot, blankets, nappies, toys! But Mary had none of these for her child.

When Jesus was born Mary wrapped him in swaddling clothes, and laid him in the manger. How simple this sounds and yet, of all the babies ever born, this one was the most important. This one was God, God who had come down to earth in the form of a little baby to be our Saviour.

After Jesus was born he received visits from two groups of people - shepherds and wise men. We can read about these visits in the Bible.

The Shepherds' Visit

Some shepherds were in the fields looking after their sheep when, suddenly, the sky was filled with light and an angel of the Lord appeared to them. The shepherds were frightened but the angel said to them, "Do not be afraid! I bring you good news. A Saviour has been born today and you will find him wrapped in swaddling clothes and lying in a manger."

Then the shepherds could hear the sound of a heavenly choir singing: "Glory to God in the highest, and peace to God's people on earth!"

The shepherds made their way to the stable to see Mary and Joseph and to worship the baby Jesus. (Luke 2:8-20)

The Wise Men's Visit

When Jesus was born in Bethlehem, he received a visit from some wise men. First they went to see King Herod and asked him, "Where will we find the baby who is the King of the Jews?

We have followed his star from the east and have come to worship him." King Herod was jealous - he didn't want anyone else to be king but himself! But he said to the wise men:

"Go and find this baby and when you have found him, come back and tell me where he is so that I can worship him myself." Herod really wanted to kill the baby Jesus.

The wise men continued to follow the star until it stopped over the place where Jesus was with Mary and Joseph. They went in and knelt down before Jesus and worshipped him. They gave him gifts of gold, frankincense and myrrh. Then they returned to their own country, having been warned in a dream not to return to Herod. (Mt 2:1-12)

The Gifts

By giving Jesus gold, the wise men were saying that they wanted Jesus to be King and Lord of their lives. The gift of frankincense was a sign that they wanted to worship Jesus as the true God. The gift of myrrh was a symbol of sorrow. With the gift of myrrh, a perfume used for the dead, the wise men were saying that Jesus had come to die to forgive our sins and lead us to God.

Activities

1. Imagine you are Mary being interviewed in Bethlehem. Write your answers to the following questions:

   (a) What is so special about your baby?

   (b) What do you think about everything that has happened to you?

   (c) How did the shepherds know where to find you?

   (d) How did the wise men know where to find you?

   (e) Why did the wise men kneel down before your baby?

2. Imagine that you are an artist who has been asked to paint a picture called 'The Birth of Jesus'!

   (a) Who will be in your picture?

   (b) Describe the different expressions you will paint on their faces.

   (c) What will be in the centre of your picture, in the background and at the sides of your picture?

   (d) Draw a simple sketch to show what your finished painting might look like.

Research

3. (a) Find out how other artists have described the birth of Jesus by looking through old Christmas cards that show the birth of Jesus.

   (b) Which is your favourite and why?

4. A crib reminds us where and how Jesus was born. Working in a small group, design and make your own simple crib.

Word Box

swaddling clothes

Jews   inn

wise men   worship

3. Called to Change

A change for the better

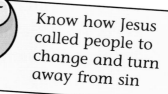

Know how Jesus called people to change and turn away from sin

When he was on earth Jesus helped many people to change their lives for the better. He helped them to stop being selfish, because being selfish only made them and other people unhappy. He showed them how they could change and how they could make things right again.

One of the people Jesus helped in this way was a man called Zacchaeus. Zacchaeus was a 'sinner' - he was selfish and did not show love to those around him. He was taking more money from people than he should have done. Read how Zacchaeus' life was changed when he met Jesus.

Picture 1

Zacchaeus was a tax-collector. He had become very rich because he was dishonest and treated people unfairly. Zacchaeus wanted to know about Jesus who was coming to his town. He was short and couldn't see anything over the heads of the crowd.

Zacchaeus climbed a tree to get a better view. As Jesus passed, he saw Zacchaeus up in the tree and said, "Come down Zacchaeus. I want to stay in your house tonight." Zacchaeus was amazed that Jesus should choose to eat in his house even though he was a sinner! He was delighted and took Jesus home and they had a wonderful meal together.

Picture 2

Picture 3

But some people in the crowd were very angry about this. They could not understand why Jesus would choose to be friends with a sinner. Zacchaeus, on the other hand, was very happy. He knew there was something amazing about Jesus, something that made him want to change and become a better person.

There and then he decided that he would not cheat people any more. He was sorry that he had ever done so. To make things right he promised to pay back all the money he had made by cheating people and to give a lot of money to the poor.

Picture 4

Zacchaeus changed when he met Jesus. He no longer sinned. Instead of thinking just about himself he thought of other people and how he could help them.

Activities

1. Look at the four pictures on these pages. They tell the story of Jesus and Zacchaeus. Look at each picture in turn and see if you can answer the questions below.

Picture 1

(a) Who do you think the crowd are looking at?

(b) Which one is Zacchaeus? How can you tell?

(c) What might Zacchaeus be thinking to himself?

Picture 2

(d) Who is looking at Zacchaeus? How do you know who this is?

(e) How can you tell that Jesus wants Zacchaeus to be his friend?

Picture 3

(f) What do you notice about the crowd?

(g) What do you think they are saying?

(h) What do you think Zacchaeus and Jesus are talking about?

Picture 4

(i) What is Zacchaeus doing?

(j) Why is he doing this?

(k) How has Zacchaeus changed?

(l) What do you think changed him?

The lost sheep

Before Zacchaeus met Jesus he was a mean and selfish man. What was it about Jesus that made Zacchaeus want to change and become a better person? Zacchaeus knew that there was something different about Jesus. He knew that Jesus wanted to be his friend even though he was a sinner.

Jesus met many people who were sinners when he was on earth. He called each of them to change their ways and become better people. He told them that God loved them very much and wanted to forgive them. Here is one story Jesus told that touched the hearts of many people he met.

There was once a shepherd who had many sheep in his flock. He loved them very much and took great care of all of them. But one day, when he was counting his sheep, he realised that one of them had gone missing. So he left his flock in the field and went off and searched all day for the one sheep that was lost.

At last, as night began to fall, he found the lost sheep alone and shivering. He was overjoyed and picked up the little sheep and carried it in his arms back to the flock. That night he called his friends and family together and said, "Let's celebrate because I have found the sheep which was lost!"

Jesus told this story because God is just like the shepherd. He loves us all very much, just as the shepherd loves his flock of sheep. Sometimes we get 'lost' – we do selfish or thoughtless things and we feel far away from God - but, like the shepherd, God will help us to come back to him.

When Jesus told stories like this one, Zacchaeus and many others realised that God loved them even though they had done wrong and that he wanted to forgive them. Just as the lost sheep was happy once the shepherd had found it, so Zacchaeus was filled with happiness when he realised that God loved him and wanted to forgive him!

 # Activities

1. **(a)** What do you think was different about the way Jesus treated people who had sinned?

(b) How do you think this made them feel?

2. **(a)** How do people know if they have done something wrong?

   (b) Suggest two ways they can show they are sorry.

3. **(a)** What does the story of 'The Lost Sheep' tell us about God?

   (b) Design a poster with the caption, 'God is my Shepherd'.

 Think about how you will illustrate your poster.

Making things right

None of us are quite like Zacchaeus but we can all think of times when we have done something wrong, been selfish or unkind and afterwards wished we could put things right again. Have you ever fallen out with a friend? Have you ever quarrelled with someone and afterwards felt really sad and wished you could make things up again?

It happened to a boy called Joe one day. Read what he wrote in his diary:

Understand the meaning of 'reconciliation'

Thursday 4th March

Dear Diary,

I've had a rotten day today. It all started at morning play when I was playing football with the others as usual. My best friend Steve kicked my football over the school fence into the road. He said sorry and I know it was an accident but at the time I just felt really angry. I shouted at him and called him stupid and then I said I'd never let him play again.

We didn't talk to each other all day and now I just feel really miserable and wish I could make everything all right again. I didn't mean any of those things I said to Steve.

What can I do to make friends with him again? What if he won't forgive me? Is there any way I can put this right?

We have all felt like this at some time or another. We have all hurt friends by saying something or doing something that causes them pain and afterwards wished we could put it right.

Well, Jesus tells us we can put it right. He tells us that if we really are sad and sorry for the wrong things we have done, we can say sorry, ask to be forgiven and try to find a way of making things right again.

Another word for making things right is **'reconciliation'**. When Joe says he wants Steve to forgive him and be his friend again, what he wants is to be reconciled with Steve. He wants to put things right between them so that they can both be happy again. Read what happened to Joe and Steve the next day:

Friday 5th March

Dear Diary,

Today was much better! Everything is sorted out between us; Steve and I are friends again.

I saw him walking ahead of me as we were going to school today and I ran to catch up with him.

I was nervous in case he just ignored me or wouldn't talk to me. I said I was sorry for yesterday and that I didn't mean what I said.

Steve was really good about it - he could have just ignored me or refused to talk to me, but he forgave me. And the best thing was, when we got to school, there was the football in the middle of the school playground. Someone must have found it in the road and thrown it back over the fence!

Activities

1. Can you think of a time when you argued with a friend?

   (a) Write your own diary entry about what happened.

   (b) Write a second diary entry about how you were both reconciled.

   (c) Do you think it's easy to forgive someone who has hurt you? Explain your answer.

2. If we argue with someone, what do you think Jesus would say we should do to put things right again?

3. Steve forgave Joe for being mean to him. What does this tell you about Steve?

The Lost son

Here is another story that Jesus told to show how much God loves us.

There was a man who had two sons and the younger son said, 'Father, give me my share of your property.' The father loved his son very much so he divided everything he had, all his money and all his property, and gave half to the younger son. Soon after, the younger son decided to leave home and his father waved goodbye to him sadly.

He travelled to a far away country. While he was there he wasted all his money having a good time and soon he had no money left. He went looking for work but the only job he could find was feeding pigs on a farm. Sometimes he was so hungry he would gladly have eaten the food the pigs ate.

One day he thought to himself, 'Even my father's servants have more to eat than I have. I know I was wrong to leave as I did and I know I hurt my father but I will go back home and tell him how sorry I am. I cannot expect him to love me again as his son, but perhaps he will give me a job as his servant.'

The son travelled home and when his father saw him coming he was filled with happiness and ran to meet him. The son said, 'I have been very selfish and I am not fit to be called your son.' But his father threw his arms around him and welcomed him into the house. 'I will have a party,' he said, 'for my son who was lost has been found.'

(Luke 15:11-32)

The Prodigal Son by Rembrandt

Activities

1. **(a)** Can you make a list of some of the selfish choices the younger son made?

   (b) How do you think the father in the story is like our Father, God?

   (c) 'This is your Life': work with two others and present the life of the younger son in three chapters, choosing one part each :-

   (i) his life at home with his family

   (ii) his life in another country

   (iii) his life back home once more. You could use words and/or pictures to help you.

   (d) Imagine you are the lost son fallen on bad times. Write a letter to your father asking him to take you back and giving reasons why he should and what you will do in return.

   Word Box
   reconciliation   forgiveness

Making things right with God

There are times when we need God's forgiveness. Sometimes we make choices that offend God, that is, when we choose to do something that we know is wrong. We feel unhappy about some of the things we have said or done, and we want to make things right with God just as Joe wanted to make things right with his friend.

Know about the Sacrament of Reconciliation as a celebration of God's love and forgiveness

The Sacrament of Reconciliation is a chance for us to do just this. It is a chance for us to make things right with God, to say sorry, and to start again. It is a chance for us to be reconciled with God.

In the Sacrament of Reconciliation we can see just how much God loves us. He loves us so much that he will forgive us for the wrong things we have done; and he doesn't forgive us just once, he forgives us over and over again, every time we receive this sacrament. In the Sacrament of Reconciliation, God offers us the grace to change our lives and to live as Jesus taught us to in the Gospels.

The Bible tells us just how much God loves us even when we turn away from him and sin:

God Says:

I have loved you ever since you were a child.
Even though you may have turned away from me,
I called you back.
It was I who taught you to walk.
I held you in my arms.
(Hosea 11:1-3)

You can see why the Sacrament of Reconciliation is such a wonderful occasion. It is a time to celebrate! Every time you receive this sacrament, you are celebrating God's great love for you!

Activities

1. Look carefully at this picture. It shows some children being unkind and hurtful to other children.

   (a) Make a list of some of the wrong things you can see being done.

   (b) Imagine you are one of the children in the picture. Write about what has happened, how you feel and how you think the other children in the picture might feel.

   (c) Why do you think some of the children in the picture might want to receive the Sacrament of Reconciliation when they have had time to think about what they have done?

2. (a) Choose your favourite lines from the writing of Hosea on page 42. Write them out and illustrate them.

   (b) What do these words tell you about God's love for you?

The Sacrament of Reconciliation

Before you receive the Sacrament of Reconciliation, ask God to help you. Think of anything you have done wrong. Were you unkind to someone? Did you say cruel or hurtful things like Joe did to his friend Steve? Ask God to forgive you.

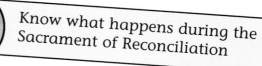

Know what happens during the Sacrament of Reconciliation

You then have a chance to tell God how sorry you are for the wrong things you have done. This is really important because you cannot be forgiven if you are not really sorry. You then say a prayer called an **Act of Sorrow**.

When you go to receive the Sacrament of Reconciliation, the priest will welcome you and ask you to tell him your sins. This is called **confession** because you are confessing or telling the priest what you have done wrong.

The priest takes the place of Jesus - he is there to listen to you and to forgive your sins. The priest will ask you to do something to show that you are really sorry and want to put things right. He may ask you to say a prayer or be kind to someone you have hurt. This is called a **penance**.

Oh my God,

because you are so good,

I am very sorry

that I have sinned against you,

and by the help of your grace,

I will not sin again.

The priest then says the words of **absolution**. You have now been reconciled with God. He has forgiven you and continues to love you as he has always done and always will do.

Activities

1. Write a set of instructions to help someone to go to confession.

2. **(a)** How do you know when you've done something wrong?

   (b) If you have done something wrong, how can you show that you are really sorry for what you have done?

   (c) Write your own Act of Sorrow or 'sorry' prayer that you could say to God.

3. Look at these pictures of people carrying out the penance that the priest has asked them to do:

   (a) Can you guess what their penance was?

   (b) Why do you think we might be asked to carry out a penance like this?

4. Match the word on the left with its correct meaning on the right.

Confession	Making things right with God and others
Penance	A special prayer to show you are sorry
Act of Sorrow	A gift offered to us by God in each sacrament we receive
Grace	Something that shows you are really sorry and want to make things right
Reconciliation	Telling the priest about the wrong things you have done

Word Box

confession   Act of sorrow
penance   absolution

Lent

Know that Lent is a time to try to change and that Ash Wednesday is the beginning of Lent

We can change for the better only when we put our trust in God to help us. **Lent** is a good time to make an extra special effort to do this. Lent lasts for forty days and ends on Easter Sunday. During this time we should remember the teaching of Jesus: to love God and to love our neighbour as ourselves.

To help them do this many people make a **Lenten Promise**.
They promise that they will do something kind or helpful or loving during Lent, so that they can show God and others how much they love them.

For example, they might promise to set aside a little time every day to talk to God in prayer; or they might promise to give up eating sweets and chocolates and put the money they save into a box for charity.

During Lent we try really hard to keep our Lenten Promise.
Remember that God loves us even if we break our promise.

The first day of Lent is called '**Ash Wednesday**' because on this day Catholics go to church to receive ashes from the priest. The priest makes the sign of the cross on our foreheads with the ash. When he does this, he invites us to **repent** for the wrongs we have done and to live the Gospel. Ashes are a sign of sorrow (penance) and remind us that one day we will die and become dust.

1. Complete these sentences with the missing words:

   (a) Lent lasts for _____ days.

   (b) Lent begins on _____ _____ and ends on _____ _____ .

   (c) To help us change for the better we can make a _____ _____ .

   (d) On _____ _____ , the priest makes the sign of the cross on our _____ with _____ _____ .
   This is a sign that we are sorry for the _____ we have done.

2. **(a)** Spend a few minutes thinking about what your Lenten Promise might be. Now write it on a piece of card folded in half.

   (b) Place your Lenten Promise in a safe place where you can look at it from time to time and remember what you have promised.

   (c) Each week during Lent, set aside a little time to ask yourself:

   (i) Has it been easy or hard to keep your promise?

   (ii) Why do you think this is?

   (iii) What has stopped you from keeping your promise?

   (iv) What has helped you to keep it?

   (v) What will you do now to make sure you try your very best to keep it?

Remember: even if you break your promise, God still loves you and wants you to keep on trying!

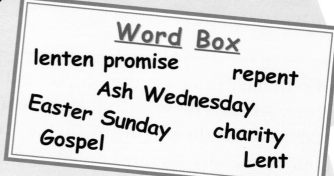

Word Box

lenten promise

repent

Ash Wednesday

Easter Sunday

Gospel

charity

Lent

4. Eucharist

Sunday - A special day!

Think about why Sunday is an important day for Christians

In the Bible we read how God asks us to keep one day each week as a special day, a day to remember all that he has done for us, a day to praise and thank him, a day to worship him.

For Christians, this special day is Sunday. Sunday is different from other days, because this is the day on which Jesus rose from death to new life. The Church remembers Jesus' resurrection every Sunday in the celebration of the **Eucharist**. By coming together to celebrate the Eucharist at Mass, we make Sunday a special day of worship.

We make Sunday a special day in other ways too. For some it is a day to spend with the family, sharing time or a meal together. Many people try not to work or shop on that day.

God said: Remember that the **Sabbath** day belongs to me. Keep it holy. You have six days for work, but the seventh day of each week belongs to me. In six days I made the sky, the earth, the oceans, everything in them, and people, but on the seventh day I rested. That's why I made the Sabbath day a special day that belongs to me. (Deuteronomy 5:12-15)

Activities

1. We have so much to thank God for. Write a 'thank you' letter to God. Name the things you want to thank him for and say why these things are important to you.

> Dear God,
>
> Just writing a note to tell you....
>
> Love from...

2. **(a)** How is Sunday a special day for you? (e.g. no school; going to play with friends etc.)

   (b) Are there any ways you can make Sunday different and show God that you love him?

3. **(a)** Here are some reasons that pupils have given for going to Mass on Sundays:

> "I go to Mass to talk to Jesus".

> "It makes me feel peaceful to go to Mass".

I want to receive Jesus in Holy Communion

(b) Think of three other reasons and write them down.

4. Find out the meaning of the words in the box and learn them.

> ## Word Box
>
> Resurrection   Sabbath
> Mass

Giving thanks to God

Think about why Catholics go to Mass

The Church asks that Catholics go to Mass once a week on Saturday evening or Sunday. Here are some of the reasons why:

We go to Mass to...

...say sorry to God

We say sorry to God for all the wrong things we have done and ask for his forgiveness.

...listen to God's Word

At Mass we listen as God speaks to us in the Bible readings.

...pray with the Church

We join our prayers with others when we thank God and praise him and ask for his help.

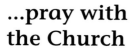

...give thanks and praise to God

We give thanks to God for all the wonderful things he has done for us.

...grow closer to Jesus

We can talk to Jesus in prayer and listen to his teachings, or stories about his life, in the Gospels. Jesus helps us most when we receive him in Holy Communion.

...be a sign to others

By coming to Mass we show others that we believe in God.

...carry on the work of Jesus

We receive strength to carry on the work of Jesus in the world and to be more like him in all we do and say.

Activities

1. Can you match the phrases on the left hand side with those on the right to make a complete sentence about why Catholics go to Mass?

   When you have finished check your sentences against the information on page 50.

We say sorry to God	in the Bible readings.
We receive Jesus in our hearts	and ask for his forgiveness.
We join our prayers with others	at Holy Communion.
We listen to God's Word	when we thank God and praise him.

2. Choose one of the sentences above.

   Design a card that expresses the thought in the sentence you've chosen.

3. Work in a small group. Together choose one reason why Catholics might go to Mass, e.g. to grow closer to Jesus. Design and make a collage to illustrate this.

Homework

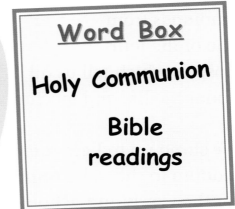

4. Conduct a survey among people you know (for example a member of your family or a friend or a teacher) to find out some of their reasons for going to Mass.

What happens at Mass

Let's take a closer look at what happens when we go to Mass.

The Mass begins with the entrance of the priest who makes the sign of the cross and welcomes everyone to the celebration.

The priest asks us to think about some of the things we have done that we are sorry for and together we ask for God's forgiveness.

Then we all join together to sing or say, a great prayer of praise and thanks to God called the 'Gloria'.

Then we listen carefully as we hear readings from the Bible.

The last reading is from one of the four Gospels which tell us all about the life and teachings of Jesus.

We stand up to hear the Gospel reading to show the respect we have for the words and actions of Jesus.

We then pray together for all the people in God's world who need our prayers. We call these prayers **Bidding Prayers**.

We want to **give thanks** to God for all the many gifts he has given us. The **Offertory** is when gifts of bread and wine are taken up to the altar as a sign that we offer ourselves to God.

The priest calls upon the Holy Spirit to change the bread and wine into the body and blood of Jesus. This is a very sacred moment and most people will kneel down.

Shortly after this we are invited to go up to the altar and receive Holy Communion. This is another very important moment in the Mass because when we receive Holy Communion we are receiving Jesus himself.

The Mass ends as the priest **blesses** us all and gives us an important **mission** - to go out into the world and serve Jesus by carrying on the work he began when he was on earth.

 # Activities

1. On a card show the order of things that happen at Mass.

2. Match the word on the left with its correct meaning on the right.

Gloria	a prayer for those in need
Gospel	the gifts of bread and wine are taken up to the altar
Bidding Prayer	a time in the Mass when we receive the body and blood of Jesus
Offertory	a book in the Bible that tells us about Jesus' life and teachings
Holy Communion	a great prayer of praise

3. (a) In your own words can you explain what this means?

> "Christ has no body now on earth but yours,
> no hands but yours."

(b) How can we carry on Jesus' work in the world after we leave Mass?

We pray together

 Become familiar with some of the prayers said during the Mass and our responses

We come to Mass to say sorry to God and ask him to forgive us for the things we have done wrong:

 May almighty God have mercy on us, forgive us our sins and bring us to everlasting life.

 Amen.

At Mass we give thanks and praise to God.

 Let us give thanks to the Lord our God.

 It is right to give Him thanks and praise.

One great prayer of praise that can be said or sung is the 'Gloria':

> **Glory to God in the highest, and peace to his people on earth.**
>
> **Lord God, heavenly King, Almighty God and Father, we worship you, we give you thanks, we praise you for your glory!**

We praise and thank God at Mass when we listen to the Bible readings.

At the end of the readings the reader reminds us:

 This is the Word of the Lord.

 Thanks be to God.

At the end of the Gospel, the priest says:

 This is the Gospel of the Lord.

And this time we reply:

 Glory to you, Lord.

To show that we want to be forgiven and are ready to forgive others and be at peace with them, the priest asks us 'to offer each other the sign of peace'.

Usually this sign is a handshake with the people who are sitting nearest to us; as we shake hands we say 'Peace be with you'.

Before we receive Holy Communion, for example, we all say the '**Lamb of God**' together:

Lamb of God, you take away the sins of the world:
have mercy on us.

Lamb of God, you take away the sins of the world:
have mercy on us.

Lamb of God, you take away the sins of the world:
grant us peace.

Activities

1. **(a)** What does the reader mean when he or she says 'This is the Word of the Lord' at the end of a reading?

    (b) Why do you think we thank God when we have heard the reading?

2. 'Peace be with you.'

    (a) Work with a partner and draw around your own and a friend's hand. You can do this in your exercise book.

    (b) Together think of ways we can spread peace in our classroom, playground or home. Write these on the hand shapes you have just drawn.

3. Your teacher will give you a copy of the words of the '**Gloria**'.

    Read it through slowly on your own and think about the words and what they mean. Now read it again.

    Choose one complete sentence to illustrate.
    Your illustration should show what you understand these words to mean.

The Body and Blood of Christ

Before Jesus died, he shared a very special meal with his friends.

Know that during the Mass the bread and wine become the body and blood of Jesus

When it was evening Jesus and his friends sat down to eat. As they were eating, Jesus took some bread, blessed it and broke it. Then he gave it to his friends saying,

"Take this all of you and eat it. This is my body."

Then Jesus took the cup of wine and again he gave it to his friends saying,

"Take this cup of wine and drink from it. This is my blood."

The Last Supper, by Leonardo da Vinci

At every Mass the priest repeats these words of Jesus:

"This is my body"

"This is the cup of my blood"

As the priest says these words the bread and wine are changed - they become the body and blood of Jesus. This means that when we receive Holy Communion, we are being offered the gift of Jesus himself.

As we receive Holy Communion, the priest will say 'The Body of Christ' and 'The Blood of Christ'. Each time we answer by saying 'Amen' - this means we are saying yes, we want to receive Jesus into our hearts because we love him and know he will help us.

This is why the time after Holy Communion is a sacred time when we can talk to Jesus in prayer.

So that Jesus remains with us in a particular way when the Mass is over, the **Blessed Sacrament** is put in a special place on or near the altar. This place is called the **tabernacle**. A red light burns beside it as a sign to us that Jesus himself is present. When we enter or leave Church, we genuflect as a mark of respect before the Blessed Sacrament.

 Activities

1. Look at the painting of the Last Supper on page 56.

   (a) What do you think this painting is about? Why?

   (b) What is happening in the painting and what are the people doing?

   (c) What do you think will happen next?

2. Imagine you are there in the painting - perhaps you are one of the characters. Write what happened that evening from your point of view.

<u>Word</u> <u>Box</u>

Blessed Sacrament

sacred   **genuflect**

tabernacle

Jesus saves us from sin

Know how Jesus died on the cross and rose again, to save us from sin

When Jesus died on the cross he was offering himself to God for all the wrong things God's people had done in the past or would do in the future. He was making things right for all of us.

Have you ever taken the blame for something someone else did? If someone did blame you for something you didn't do, you'd probably cry out, "It's not fair!" But Jesus didn't say, "It's not fair." Instead he let himself be taken away and nailed onto a wooden cross. He gave his life to make up for all the wrong things everybody else did. At the end of Lent the Church remembers how Jesus gave up his life for us, and how he rose from the dead, in the celebrations of **Holy Week**.

On **Holy Thursday** we remember how Jesus shared the Last Supper with his friends. When the meal had ended, Jesus and his friends went to a quiet place to pray. It was then that one of Jesus' friends, a man called Judas, betrayed Jesus. "The one I shall kiss is the man you want," he told Jesus' enemies. So, when he saw Jesus, he went up to him and greeted him with a kiss and Jesus' enemies arrested him and took him away.

On **Good Friday** the Church remembers how Jesus loved us so much he gave up his life for us and died on the cross.
This is called his '**Passion**'.

He was crucified between two criminals. One of them shouted at him and said, "If you really are God's son, why don't you save yourself, and us!" But the other criminal saw that there was something different about Jesus, and he called out, "Jesus, remember me when you come into your kingdom." And Jesus promised him, "Do not worry, today you will be with me in heaven!"

Because of the way Jesus died for us, the cross has become a very special and beautiful sign for Christians. Many churches are built in the shape of a cross; we often make the sign of the cross when we want to pray. The cross reminds us of the great love Jesus has for us, so great that he gave his life to make up for our sins.

 # Activities

1. Can you think of a time when you were blamed for something you didn't do?

    (a) Write or draw about this time.

    (b) How did you feel when you were unfairly blamed?

    (c) Do you think it was fair that Jesus died on the cross for our sins?

    (d) What does this tell you about the sort of person Jesus was?

2. Read the piece of Scripture opposite.

    (a) What do you think Jesus meant?

    (b) How did Jesus prove his love for us?

> Jesus said: "A man can have no greater love than this, that he lays down his life for his friends."
> (John 15:13)

3. **(a)** Draw your own crucifix in the centre of a page.

    (b) Now write or draw around it some of the important events of Holy Week.

Easter Sunday

As well as reminding us of Jesus' death and how much he loved us, the cross reminds us of something else too. It reminds us that after Jesus' body had been taken down from the cross and laid in a tomb, something wonderful happened. Do you remember what this was? Read the story below and find out!

Know that Jesus rose from the dead on Easter Sunday

Very early one morning, just after the sun had risen, Mary Magdalene and some other women went to the tomb of Jesus. When they got there they were amazed to see that the large stone blocking the entrance to the tomb had been rolled away!

They rushed inside and saw an angel dressed all in white.

He said to them, "Do not be afraid. You are looking for Jesus but he is not here. He has risen. Go and tell his friends what has happened. They will see Jesus again!"

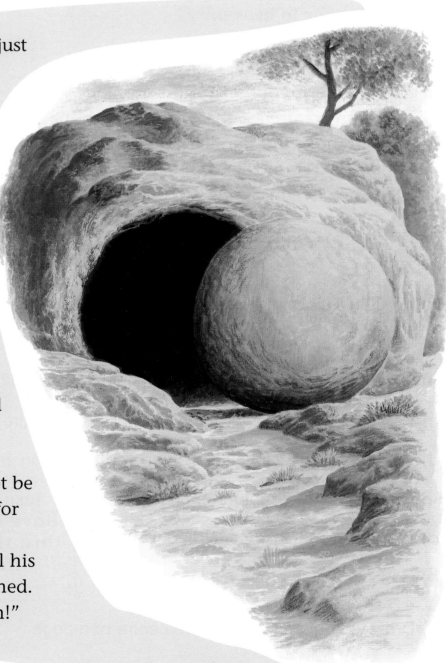

On Easter Sunday the Church celebrates the most wonderful thing ever to happen. Jesus has risen! Even though Jesus died on the cross, God raised him from death to new life. This is called his 'Resurrection'. And we believe that, one day, God will raise us to new life too, so that we can live with him forever in heaven. Jesus also wants to raise us up to new life every day as well - to keep us close to him.

 # Activities

1. Now you can finish your cross.

Write something that will remind you of the wonderful event we celebrate on Easter Sunday.

2. Year 1 pupils have not heard the story of what happened on Holy Thursday, Good Friday and Easter Sunday.

Write down the story for them using words and pictures.

Tell them:

(a) Who Jesus was with on Holy Thursday?

(b) Who betrayed Jesus?

(c) What happened on Good Friday?

(d) What happened on Easter Sunday?

(e) Who was the first to hear about it?

3. Imagine you are one of the women visiting the tomb of Jesus. Write about what happened.

(a) Describe how you felt when you set off to the tomb;

(b) what you saw when you got there;

(c) how you felt when you heard what the angel had to say.

4. Write a poem or design a poster with the title: He is Risen!

Word Box

angels   Mary Magdalene

tomb   heaven

crucifix   scripture

5. Celebrating Easter & Pentecost

Celebrating new life

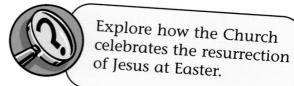

Explore how the Church celebrates the resurrection of Jesus at Easter.

Spring

Winter is over.
The world is waking up
from its deep sleep.

The bare tree is now clothed,
the daffodil raises its golden head,
the sharp wind is conquered by
the gentle breeze.

And once again the Creator
has restored life
to a sleeping world.

Have you ever noticed some of the changes around us after a long winter? The weather changes and we don't have to wear gloves or scarves or even coats as we travel to school in the mornings. The evenings become brighter. The bare trees are gradually covered in leaves, and flowers and plants begin to appear. During springtime, the world begins to wake up from its long winter sleep and come to life again.

At Easter the Church celebrates a very special feast about coming to life again - the resurrection of Jesus! Easter is the most important feast that we celebrate in the whole year.

This is because on Easter Sunday we celebrate Jesus' resurrection from the dead. Even though Jesus suffered and died on the cross, his resurrection shows that God's power is greater than death. God raised Jesus from death to new life.

The cross on the candle reminds us that Jesus died and rose again to new life; **A** and **Ω** are the beginning and end of the Greek alphabet, they remind us that the risen Jesus will live forever.

Easter begins with the **Easter Vigil** late on **Holy Saturday**, after night has fallen, when a special Mass is held in church. The service begins with the lighting of the Easter or **Paschal** candle, to remind us that Jesus, our light, is risen.

The next day, Easter Sunday, another joyful Mass is celebrated. All the prayers and readings on this wonderful day remind us that Jesus has passed from death to new life:

Christ has died.

Christ is risen.

Christ will come again!

 # Activities

1. Read the poem "Spring" on page 62 and answer the following questions:

   (a) What signs of new life in spring are mentioned in the poem?

   (b) What other signs of new life have you noticed in springtime?

   (c) Make a list of all the things you enjoy about springtime.

   (d) Who do you think the 'Creator' in the poem is?

   (e) Explain the last two lines of the poem in your own words.

   (f) In what way is Easter a celebration of new life?

2. As the Paschal Candle is lit the priest says the following prayer:

   > **May the light of Christ,**
   >
   > **rising in glory,**
   >
   > **dispel the darkness**
   >
   > **of our hearts and minds.**

   (a) Draw a candle and write the words in the box around your candle.

   (b) How is Jesus a 'light' for Christians?

   (c) How can we be a 'light' to others?

3. Imagine you have been asked to explain Easter to someone who has never heard of this feast before. Write a letter, using pictures and words, and include the following points:

(a) What we celebrate at Easter.

(b) Why Easter is the most important feast in the Church's year.

(c) How Easter is celebrated in Church.

(d) Why the Paschal candle is lit.

3. (a) Design a 'Happy Easter' card.

Dear ....

Thank you for your letter ....

On Easter Sunday..............

Love from ....

(b) Try to put a drawing on it that shows the real meaning of Easter.

(c) On the inside write a few words to remind people that it is an occasion for a big celebration, for example, "Rejoice!..."

The Resurrection, by Piero della Francesca

<u>**Word Box**</u>

Creator

Holy Saturday

Easter Vigil

feast

He is risen!

This story shows us how the despair of Jesus' friends changed to happiness when they saw Jesus was truly alive!

A walk with Jesus

Two of Jesus' friends were walking along the road from Jerusalem to a village called Emmaus. They felt sad and confused and talked about all that had happened - how Jesus had died on the cross, had been laid in a tomb, and how the tomb had been found empty.

Jesus appeared and walked alongside them, but they did not recognise him!

"What are you talking about?" Jesus asked. They looked at him sadly, "Haven't you heard about what has happened in Jerusalem over the past few days, about the death of Jesus of Nazareth, and how some women went to his tomb and say they found it empty? They even say they saw an angel there who told them Jesus has risen!"

Jesus said, "O foolish people, why are you so slow to believe that Jesus really did die and has risen again?" He explained to them that all this happened just as the Scriptures said it would. As they listened to him they began to feel much happier. They asked Jesus to stay and have supper with them. When they were eating, Jesus took the bread and blessed it, and broke it, and gave it to them. As he did this they recognised him, and then he vanished from their sight. They said to each other, "It was Jesus! He really is alive!" with their hearts full of joy. (Luke 24:13-35)

In the story Jesus 'vanished from their sight', but this did not make the two friends sad again - they could no longer see Jesus but they knew he was still with them and would always be with them. It is the same for us - we cannot see Jesus in the same way as we can see other people, but that does not mean he is not there. He has risen to new life he will always be with us.

- He is with us when we pray - we can talk to Jesus anytime we want to and he will be there ready to listen to us.
- He is with us when we read his teachings in the Bible.
- When we go to Mass he is with us in a special way in the Eucharist.
- He is present in every person we meet - Jesus said, 'Whatever you do to my brothers and sisters, you do to me'.

Activities

1. Imagine you are one of Jesus' two friends in the story above. Write down what you told Jesus' other friends when you got back to Jerusalem.

2. Copy and complete this chart. Fill in the missing words and draw pictures to show each way Jesus is still with us:

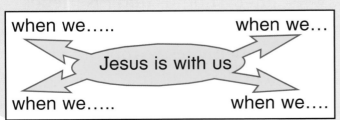

3. (a) What do you think Jesus meant by these words?

"Whatever you do to my brothers and sisters, you do to me." (Matt 25:40)

(b) Can you think of one way you can put these words of Jesus into practice today?

Celebrating Jesus' love for us

We have seen how happy Jesus' friends were when they realised that Jesus had risen. As well as happiness, they must have felt amazement and wondered how such a thing could be possible.

Know that because Jesus rose from death to new life, we have hope that we will too

One of Jesus' friends, a man called Thomas, heard about the empty tomb and how people were saying Jesus had risen, but he just couldn't believe it was true.

Doubting Thomas

One of Jesus' close friends was a man called Thomas. He had really loved Jesus and when Jesus died Thomas felt very sad. When Thomas' friends told him that Jesus' tomb was empty, and that some of them had actually seen Jesus, he couldn't believe it. He wished it were true because he really missed Jesus, but he felt that such a thing was not possible. How could someone who had died be alive again? It just didn't make sense!

Thomas said to his friends, "I will not believe Jesus has risen unless I see him for myself!" About a week later, Thomas and his friends were in their house with all the doors shut. Suddenly Jesus appeared in the middle of the room and said, "Peace be with you".

Thomas was amazed - could that really be Jesus who he loved so much and thought he would never see again? Jesus came to Thomas and spoke to him, "Why do you doubt Thomas? Can you see the marks on my hands from the nails on the cross? Believe that it is me."

And Thomas realised that it really was Jesus, and that he had risen to new life. He cried out, "Jesus, my Lord and my God!"
Jesus replied, "You believe because you have seen me. Blessed are those who have not seen me and yet they believe in me." (John 20:24-29)

Jesus knew that some people, like Thomas, might find it hard to believe that Jesus would die, but then rise again. So he told his friends a story to help them understand what was going to happen to him.

He said that it was a bit like planting a grain of wheat in the ground. First the seed has to be buried in the dark earth.

No one can see it and no one knows what is happening to it.

But soon little, tiny shoots will appear above the ground and the plant will grow and grow, until everyone can see that it has become a strong, tall stalk of wheat.

This is what happened to Jesus. When he died on the cross, friends took his body and laid him in a tomb. They felt very sad because they thought that this was the end and they wouldn't see Jesus again. But just as the little seed rises out of the darkness to enjoy new life as a beautiful flower, so Jesus rose from the dead - he came back to a new life. And this is what we believe will happen to us too one day.

Jesus' resurrection gives us hope that when we die, God will raise us to new life as well, and that we will live forever with Jesus and his Father in the kingdom of heaven.

Jesus himself promised this to his followers when he was on earth:

> **In my Father's house there**
>
> **are many rooms.**
>
> **I am going first to prepare**
>
> **a place for you.**
>
> **One day I will come back for you,**
>
> **so that where I am,**
>
> **you may be also.** (John 14:2-3)

We also believe that Jesus' resurrection gives us hope every day that he is always close to us and is looking after us - giving us the same new life that he has.

 ## Activities

1. Work with a partner.

   Imagine you are a reporter for the 'Jerusalem Times' and that you have been sent along to interview Thomas about his experience.

   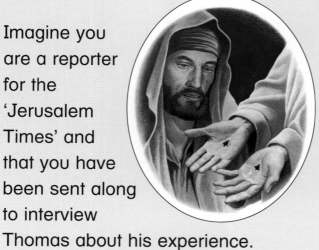

   (a) Write a list of questions that you would like to ask Thomas about what happened and how he came to believe in Jesus' resurrection.

   (b) Now imagine you are Thomas and write your answers to these questions.

2. **(a)** Tell the story of the grain of wheat using pictures and words.

(b) Why do you think Jesus told his friends this story?

(c) What hope does this story give us?

(d) In your own words can you explain the promise Jesus made to his followers?

3. Work in groups...

(a) Chose one of the stories of Jesus appearing to his friends.

    (i) The Emmaus Story (Page 66).
    or
    (ii) Doubting Thomas (Page 68).

(b) Write this story as a little play.

    (i) How many characters will you need?

    (ii) Who are they?

    (iii) Write down what each person will say.

    (v) Chose one person to introduce the story.

(c) Practice your story and then present it to the rest of the class.

3. Work in pairs to make a poster for the school entrance or your church to remind everybody about what we are celebrating at Easter.

Celebrating Pentecost

Have you ever had a problem that you couldn't solve on your own, but someone came along and helped you to solve it?

Perhaps you did not understand something in class and a teacher explained it to you.
Or maybe you've been a help to someone else, cheering up a friend who felt unhappy?
The truth is we all need a helping hand at one time or another.

Jesus' friends were the same. They were happy that Jesus had risen to new life. But they were unsure about what they should do next and how they should carry on the work Jesus had begun when he was on earth. They needed someone to help them. Then, one day, that help came - Jesus sent the **Holy Spirit** to be their helper, and changed their lives forever.

On the day of **Pentecost**, Jesus' friends were together in one room. A strong wind began to blow and it filled the room with its mighty roar. They saw tongues of fire come down and rest upon their heads and they were filled with the Holy Spirit.

Suddenly they no longer felt unsure about what they should do. They knew they had to spread the good news that Jesus had told them. They went out to tell everyone they met all about Jesus and his teachings. Many people who heard them wanted to join them.

Every year, on the feast of **Pentecost**, the Church remembers how the Holy Spirit was sent to help the friends of Jesus. This is a very important feast because, without the Holy Spirit, the friends of Jesus would never have had the courage or the confidence to carry on the work Jesus had begun. If that had happened, many people might never have heard of Jesus. In the same way, the Holy Spirit helps us to be like Jesus and to carry on his work.

Activities

1. **(a)** Write or draw about a time someone gave you help when you needed it.

   (b) Write down how you can be of help to someone today.

2. Imagine you were one of the friends of Jesus in the room when the Holy Spirit came. Write about what happened - what you saw, heard or felt - and explain how the Holy Spirit changed you.

3. On the day of Pentecost the Holy Spirit came like rushing wind and burning fire.

   (a) Design a Pentecost banner, which includes one or both of these symbols.

   (b) If you want to, you can add some wording to your banner - perhaps choose a line from a hymn to the Holy Spirit.

   (c) When you have designed your banner, you could make it using different materials.

Pentecost Banner

The power of the Holy Spirit

The Holy Spirit came to help the friends of Jesus and that includes you and me! The Spirit is alive in each of us. We know the Holy Spirit is alive in people whenever they do and say things that show God's Spirit of love, joy and peace. And people know the Holy Spirit is alive in *us* whenever we act in a kind and caring way.

Reflect on times when we need the help of the Holy Spirit

The Holy Spirit can help us to change, just like the friends of Jesus changed on the day of Pentecost. **St Paul** once wrote a letter to some of his Christian friends encouraging them to live by the Spirit because:

'The fruit of the Spirit is love, joy, peace, patience, kindness, goodness, faithfulness, gentleness, and self-control'.

By this he meant that if we let the Holy Spirit work in us, as it worked in Jesus' friends on the day of Pentecost, then we would have all these good qualities.

LOVE
JOY
PEACE
PATIENCE
GOODNESS
KINDNESS
SELF-CONTROL
GENTLENESS
FAITHFULNESS

There are times when we all need a helping hand to be the good Christians we have been called to be. The Holy Spirit is always there to help us. When we find it hard to be kind or to forgive someone, when we don't want to share with others or let someone join in our games, when we are about to lose our temper, - these are all times we can call on the Holy Spirit and ask for help.

 **Activities**

1. **(a)** In the middle of your page write the words,

   The Spirit lives in me when….

   (b) Draw speech bubbles around these words like this.

The Spirit lives in me when...

   (c) Think about things that you can do or say that will show others the Holy Spirit is alive in you for example "I share my things with others". Then write these in the bubbles.

2. **(a)** Draw a flame shape on card and cut it out.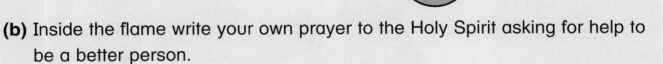

   (b) Inside the flame write your own prayer to the Holy Spirit asking for help to be a better person.

3. Work in a small group.

   (a) Together select one fruit of the Spirit, for example 'love'.

   (b) Prepare a presentation (e.g. a poster or a play etc) for the class on the fruit you have chosen, and how it can help you to be a better person.

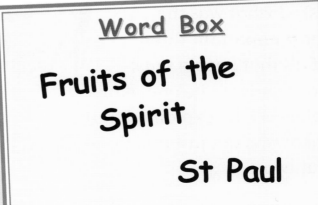

Word Box

Fruits of the Spirit

St Paul

6. Being a Christian
Loving God and each other

When we received the Sacrament of Baptism the Holy Spirit came to live in us and we became part of the Christian family known as the Church. Being a Christian means that we should try to live our lives in the way Jesus taught us when he was on earth.

Think about what being a Christian means

Jesus was kind to everybody. He was always ready to forgive people when they had done wrong. He went about doing what he could to help others, to comfort the lonely, to cure the sick and to work miracles so that people would believe in the power of God.

When Jesus was asked what was the most important thing of all that people must do in order to be one of his followers, he explained that there was not just one thing, but two:

"This is the first," Jesus said: "Listen, the Lord our God is the one Lord, and you must love the Lord your God with all your heart, with all your soul, with all your mind and with all your strength." (Mark 12:29-30)

"The second is this: You must love your neighbour as yourself." (Mark 12:31)

One day Peter asked Jesus how often he should forgive somebody who does something wrong to him. Without waiting for Jesus to reply, he said, what if that person hurts me again and again, should I forgive him seven times. Here is what Jesus said:

"Not seven, I tell you, but seventy-seven times." (Matt 18:22)

Jesus is telling us that we must always love God, love one another and always be ready to forgive each other when we do something wrong.

Activities

1. What do you think being a Christian involves? Try to think of three things.

2. Do you think it is easy being a Christian? Explain your answer.

3. (a) Read or listen to the story of **The Good Samaritan.** (Luke 12:29-37)

   (b) Draw pictures to go with the story and use speech bubbles to show what the people in the story are saying.

St Peter

Life is not always easy; sometimes it is great and other times difficult. This was certainly true for one of Jesus' greatest friends, Peter.
Read about some of the good and bad times in Peter's life below.

Know how St Peter became a follower of Jesus

Jesus calls Peter
Peter was a fisherman who made a living by taking his boat out every day onto the lake, and throwing his net into the water to catch fish. But one day something happened that was to change his simple life forever - he met Jesus!

On this day, as he and his brother Andrew cast their nets into the water, Jesus called out to them, "Follow me and you will become fishers of men!"

Peter did not hesitate. It was as if he knew there was something different, something special about Jesus.

Immediately he dropped his nets and went with Jesus. (Mark 1:16-18)

Peter makes a promise

On the night that Jesus was arrested, he warned his friends about the difficult times they would face in the days ahead. Peter loved him so much, he couldn't bear to hear Jesus talk so sadly.

He promised, "I will never let you down Jesus, even if everyone else does!"

But Jesus replied, "Peter, you will let me down three times before this night is ended."

Peter was shocked. How could Jesus even think of such a thing! Jesus was his best friend - of course Peter would never let him down!

"Even if I must die with you," he promised Jesus, "I will never let you down." (Matthew 26:33-35)

Peter breaks his promise

After Jesus had been arrested, Peter followed from a distance and watched as Jesus was taken to the house of the High Priest. While Jesus was taken inside, Peter remained outside in the courtyard warming himself at a fire with some others.

As he waited there, a maid recognised him and called out, "You are a friend of the man called Jesus." But Peter denied it. "I don't know him," he said.

A little later, a man saw him and also recognised him, "You are one of those who follow Jesus!" And again Peter denied it, 'I am not' he said.

About an hour later, someone else called out, "You're one of the friends of the man who's been arrested!"

As Peter denied this yet again, he heard a cock crow and realised the night was ending. He remembered Jesus' words, "Peter, you will let me down three times before this night is ended."

Jesus was right. Peter had let him down, not once, but three times. Peter went out of the courtyard and wept sadly. (Luke 21:54-62)

However, that is not the end of the story.

Jesus had said that no matter how often a person has hurt us, we must always be ready to forgive them. He loved Peter and not only did he forgive him for letting him down badly three times, but he made him a very famous person. Peter became the head of the Church!

Peter learnt how to overcome his fears and doubts.

With the help of Jesus he went on to lead an amazing life, and to have many adventures as he travelled around telling others about Jesus. Peter went around baptising people and telling them how Jesus had risen from the dead, and had made it possible for them to enjoy **eternal life** with him in heaven.

 # Activities

1. **(a)** Imagine you are a fisherman who was there on the day that Jesus asked Peter to follow him.

    In your own words describe what happened.

    (b) What do you think Jesus meant when he said that Peter would be a 'fisher of men'?

2. How do you think Peter felt when he heard the cock crow?

3. What do you think Peter will remember most about the different things that happened to him?

Word Box	
denied	eternal life

St Paul

Understand how St Paul had to learn to be a Christian

Paul was another great follower of Jesus who, like Peter, faced many challenges in his life but, unlike Peter, he never actually met Jesus. In fact, to begin with, Paul really hated Christians until one day something happened to change him...

There was once a man called Saul who did everything he could to hurt Christians. He thought that they were just troublemakers and he did not believe in the teachings of Jesus. One day, he went to the town of Damascus searching for Christians he could arrest and throw into prison.

Near Damascus, a bright light suddenly shone all around him and he heard a voice say to him, "Saul, Saul, why do you persecute me?" Saul was surprised and asked who it was. The voice replied, "I am Jesus and you are persecuting me. Get up now and go into the city and you will be told what to do."

Saul was left blinded - he could see nothing! His friends took him by the hand to a house in the city. After a few days, a Christian called Ananias came to visit him. He healed Saul's blindness and when Saul realised that it was Jesus who had spoken to him on the road to Damascus, he wanted to change and become a Christian too. (Acts 9:1-19)

From that day on Saul changed from being an enemy of Jesus, to being one of his greatest followers. To show that he was no longer the man he had once been, he changed his name to Paul and spent the rest of his life spreading the good news of Jesus!

At first Paul was very puzzled about what Jesus said: "I am Jesus and you are persecuting me". Paul knew he was persecuting Christians but he could not understand how he was persecuting Jesus. Ananias explained to him how Jesus is present in Christians. Eventually Paul understood that whatever we do to each other, we do to Jesus.

Activities

1. If you interviewed St Paul, what questions would you ask him about his experience on the road to Damascus?

   (a) Write down your questions.

   (b) Write down what you think St Paul might say in reply to each question.

3. Imagine you are Saul. Design a 'WANTED' poster for Christians, explaining why you want them captured and what 'crime' they have committed.

4. What do you think were the most important lessons that St Paul had to learn in order to become a true follower of Jesus?

2. Here is part of a letter that St Paul wrote to Christians who lived in the town of Corinth:

Love is patient and kind,
love is not jealous or boastful,
it is not arrogant or rude.
Love does not insist on its own way,
it is not irritable or resentful...

   (a) Explain two of the phrases which you like best in your own words.

   (b) Write your own 'Love is...' poem.

You are unique

Think about your gifts and talents

No two people are exactly the same. Peter and Paul were very different. God has created us so that we are all different from each other. Each of us is special, unique. If you look around you, you will see that there is no-one else in the class who is exactly like you: you all look different from each other. You have different voices, different personalities, different skills and abilities.

God has given us many gifts, such as our **senses** - sight, touch, taste, hearing and smell. God has given us these gifts so that we can enjoy living in the world that he has created for us.

For the gift of sight

I thank you, Lord
- That I can see the glorious golden sunrise at dawn and watch the burning raging sun set on a summer's day.

For the gift of hearing

I thank you, Lord
- That I can hear the wind whistling over the moors and the sound of the waves as they crash on the shore.

For the gift of touch

I thank you, Lord - That I can feel the soft warm fur of the cats as they curl up on my lap and feel the golden grains of sand as they slide through my fingers.

For the gift of smell

I thank you, Lord
- That I can catch the faint aroma of my mother's perfume and the heady scent of roses in the garden.

For the gift of taste

I thank you, Lord - That I can enjoy the sharp sting of a lemon and the sweet juice of an apple as it dribbles down my chin!

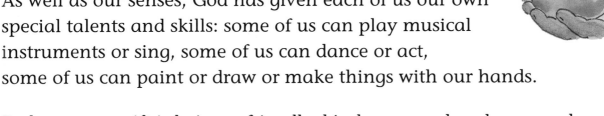

As well as our senses, God has given each of us our own special talents and skills: some of us can play musical instruments or sing, some of us can dance or act, some of us can paint or draw or make things with our hands.

Perhaps your gift is being a friendly, kind person who always makes other people laugh and smile; or maybe you can write really interesting stories or lovely poems. Maybe your gift is with computers or roller skates or a football.

Activities

1. Write a letter to an imaginary friend. Tell them everything you want to say about yourself:

   (a) what you look like,

   (b) what your likes and dislikes are,

   (c) what your gifts and talents are,

   (d) what you enjoy doing,

   (e) what makes you unique.

2. **(a)** Think about the senses God has given you, and how these make your life enjoyable.

   (b) Draw a chart in your book with the name of your senses in one column and in the other write the things you most enjoy with that sense, for example:-

Senses	What I enjoy
Hearing	Listening to music

   (c) Choose one of the five senses and write your own senses poem.

3. Copy and complete this chart:

My gifts and talents	How I can use it to bring happiness to others

God's gifts to us

Be aware of the graces we receive through the sacraments

This has been a very important year for each one of us. We now understand that through the Sacrament of Baptism we became Christians and members of the Catholic Church.

In the Sacrament of Reconciliation, when we go to Confession, we receive God's forgiveness for anything we have done wrong. No matter how often we fail, God offers us the grace to change our lives and to live as Jesus taught us in the Gospels. We can receive the Sacrament of Reconciliation every time we have done anything wrong and want God to help us.

When we make our First Holy Communion, we receive the Sacrament of the Eucharist. Each time we go to Mass, when we receive Holy Communion we receive Jesus. He becomes truly present in us so that we are able to talk to him and ask for his help to live the way he want us to and share in his life.

In the **Sacrament of Baptism** Jesus joins us to his Christian family, the Church.

In the **Sacrament of Reconciliation** Jesus helps us to change our lives and to love one another.

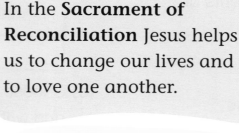

In the **Sacrament of the Eucharist**, Jesus comes to us in Holy Communion.

Read what these children have to say about the gifts they have received.

When I received Holy Communion for the very first time I felt loved. I thought Jesus was giving me a present when he gave me himself in the bread and wine. **Sarah - age 7**

My happiest memory this year was my first Holy Communion.
I received Jesus for the first time. This made me very happy and I know Jesus will always be my friend. All my family came with me to the Church. It was a very special day for me. **Sam - age 8**

When I went to confession for the first time, I was really nervous but I was excited as well. I was scared that I wouldn't remember what to say. But the priest helped me. Whenever I go to confession, I feel so happy Jesus loves me.
Stefan - age 7

For these children, their happiest day was the day they received a sacrament for the first time. In every sacrament we receive, God offers us the gift of his life. This is the grace we need to help us on our journey through life. Every time we receive a sacrament, we are reminded that God is with us. He will never leave us!

 # Activities

1. Think about the past school year

   (a) Draw a road and divide it up into twelve sections and write the months of the year in each section.

   (b) In the right month, record the most important events that happened to you (your birthday, First Holy Communion).

   (c) What was the happiest thing that happened to you this year? Plot it on your road, then write about what happened and how you felt.

2. **(a)** Why were Sam and Stefan so happy when they received the Sacraments?

   (b) What gifts or graces has God offered you in the sacraments you have received so far?

   (c) How might these gifts help you to be a good Christian?

I have a dream

Reflect on how you will use the gifts God has given you to be a good Christian

Do you ever wonder what the future will be like? Do you ever wonder what the world will be like in ten, twenty, thirty or a hundred years from now?

Do you ever think about what you will do with your life, what you will achieve, what difference you will make to others?

We all have our hopes and dreams for the future, for ourselves, for our families and for the world. Read some of the dreams young people have had.

My dream for the future...

I am going to be a famous astronaut and fly to the moon. **Brian Age 6**

I hope everyone will be much kinder to each other and there will be no more fighting or war. **Elise Age 8**

I want my mum and my brother to be happy and not worry about things any more. **Marinder Age 7**

What are your dreams? Remember God is with you every step of the way. He is always at your side. With God's love you can do anything, be anyone, achieve everything!

Activities

1. **(a)** Copy and complete the chart below.

My hopes and dreams...			
...for myself	...for my family	...for my friends	...for the world

(b) How can you use your gifts and talents to make these dreams come true?

(c) Write your own speech that begins 'I have a dream...'

2. Research the life of one person who tried to make the world a better place for others? For example: Mother Theresa.

My Goals

3. **(a)** Look at the table below.

(b) Fill in the boxes with your plans for next year.

Help Box

Goal = Something you want to do, such as to work hard at school

Steps to be taken = What you need to do to achieve your goal

Target time = How long it is going to take

Name:		What I would like to do:	
	Goal	Steps to be taken	Target time
Home			
School			
My Faith			
Friends			
Hobbies			

Glossary

Absolution - In the Sacrament of Reconciliation when the priest, in the place of Jesus, 'absolves', forgives, your sins

Act of sorrow - A prayer to say how sorry we are for our sins

Angels - They live with God in heaven, singing his praise; some are sent as messengers, like Gabriel

Angel Gabriel - The angel whom God sent to Mary

Annunciation - When Gabriel brought God's message to Mary that he wanted her to be the mother of his son, Jesus

Anointed - To pour a special oil onto someone

Ash Wednesday - The first day of Lent, when we receive the ash on our foreheads

Baptised - When a person receives the Sacrament of Baptism they are baptised

Baptismal candle - The candle given to the newly baptised child

Baptismal font - The place in a church containing the blessed water poured onto someone when they are baptised

Baptismal garment - The white dress or shawl which is put on or wrapped around a newly baptised child during baptism

Baptismal promises - The promises which the parents and godparents make for the child during baptism

Baptismal water - The holy water used to baptise someone

Bible Readings - Usually short stories from the Bible which are read in church, for example during Mass

Bishop - A person who is in charge of all the people and churches in his area

Blessed Sacrament - The body of Jesus, in the form of a consecrated host which is kept in the tabernacle

Celebrate - To rejoice and be happy, and to do something special

Charity - To do something kind to someone

Christian Name - The name you receive when you are baptised, and usually is a person's first name

Church - Name of the building where Catholics worship and go to Mass

Commandments - These are also called 'words of life', instructions which God gave to us

Confession - In the Sacrament of Reconciliation when you tell the priest your sins

Creator - A name given to God because he is the one who has made or 'created' everything

Crucifix - A cross with the figure of Jesus on it

Denied - To have told a lie, say the opposite of the truth on purpose

Easter Sunday - The day when Jesus rose from the dead

Easter Vigil - The night before Easter Sunday, when Christians celebrate the death and resurrection of Jesus

Eternal Life - The life with God in heaven which Christians hope to have forever after they die

Eucharist - Another word for the Mass, and it comes from a foreign word (Greek) meaning 'giving thanks'

Feast - A special day when Christians celebrate something important in Jesus' life, or Mary's life, or one of the Saints. Also called a Feast day

Forgiveness - When someone forgives someone else, pardons or lets them off

Fruits of the Spirit - Gifts from God

Genuflect - To go down on the right knee, as a sign of reverence, for example before the tabernacle in Church

Godparent - Someone who promises to help bring a baptised person up as a Christian

Gospel - This means 'good news', and is the story of the life of Jesus

Grace - A help or gift which comes from God

Hail Mary - A prayer to Our Lady, Mary the mother of Jesus

Heaven - Where God lives, with Jesus, Mary and all the saints

Holy Communion - The bread and wine that has been changed into the body and blood of Jesus, which we receive at Mass

Holy Saturday - The day before Easter Sunday

Holy Spirit - Third Person of the Blessed Trinity

Icon - A holy painting, usually of Jesus, Mary or the Saints, often seen in churches

Inn - A place where travellers could have food and rest

Jews - The 'people of Israel'. These are God's chosen people and their story is in the Bible

Lent - Forty days of preparing for Easter. It starts on Ash Wednesday

Lenten promise - A promise to change for the better, which we can make at the start of Lent

Marriage - When a man and a woman are 'married' in Church as husband and wife

Mary Magdalene - One of Jesus' followers

Mass - The Sacrament of the Eucharist

Nazareth - The small town where Jesus lived and grew up

Parish - The area Catholics live in where they have their Church and a priest to look after them

Parish Church - The Church in your parish where you go to Mass and receive the sacraments

Parish priest - The priest who is in charge of a Church and the Catholics in a local area

Paschal candle - The large candle which is lit at Easter

Penance - A prayer or something else to show we want to make things right with God, or others we have hurt

Prophet - A holy person in the Bible, who wrote down or told people all about God

Reconciliation - The sacrament we receive when we confess and receive forgiveness for our sins

Repent - To be sorry for the wrong things you have done and to want God's forgiveness

Resurrection - When Jesus, who had died, was raised up to new life by God his Father, on Easter Sunday

Rite of Baptism - The words and signs used when a person is baptised

Sabbath - The holy day every week when the Jews rested from work and blessed God (a Saturday)

Sacrament - A very important gift from Jesus, when we receive special help and grace

Sacred - This means holy, or special to God

Saviour - A name given to Jesus, because he died and rose again to 'save' everyone from sin and death

Scripture - Another word for the writings in the Bible

St Paul - A famous follower of Jesus. He died for being Christian

St Peter - One of the Apostles of Jesus. He died for being a Christian

Statue - A figure of a person carved out of stone or wood

Swaddling clothes - Clothes to wrap around a new born baby

Tabernacle - The place where the Blessed Sacrament is kept in the church

Tomb - A place where someone is buried

Visitation - The time when Mary went to visit her cousin Elizabeth

Wise Men - Also known as the 'Magi' or 'Kings', they made a very long journey to visit the baby Jesus

Worship - To adore, respect, praise

Nihil obstat: Father Anton Cowan (Censor).

Imprimatur: The Very Rev. Alan Hopes, V.G., Westminster, 29 April 2002.

The Nihil obstat *and* Imprimatur *are a declaration that the book or pamphlet is considered to be free from doctrinal or moral error. It is not implied that those who have granted the* Nihil obstat *and the* Imprimatur *agree with the contents, opinions or statements expressed.*

Published 2002 by The Incorporated Catholic Truth Society,

40-46 Harleyford Road,

London SE1 5AY

Tel: 020 7640 0042   Fax: 020 7640 0046

website: www.cts-online.org.uk

ISBN: 1 86082 164 2   CTS Code: Pr 02

Designed and Produced by: The Catholic Truth Society/Stephen Campbell.

Picture research: The Catholic Truth Society/Pierpaolo Finaldi.

Front cover: The Holy Family © Adrian Barclay/ Beehive Illustration.

Printed by: Arkle Print Limited.

Acknowledgments

Considerable thanks are due to the teachers in the following schools who contributed to the development of this Pupil Book 3 by way of advice, editorial review and comment. The Way the Truth and the Life series has been a collaborative exercise: kind thanks are expressed in particular to the following schools: Farleigh School, Andover; Notre Dame School, Greenwich; Our Lady of Lourdes School, Barnet; Sacred Heart School, Barnet; St Teresa's School, Harrow; St Agnes' School, Barnet; St Vincent's School, Barnet; St Margaret Clitherow School, Brent; St Mary School, Brent; St Raphael's School, Ealing.

Editorial Team

Louise McKenna, Amette Ley, Elizabeth Redmond, Anthony O'Rourke, Laura Lamb, Fergal Martin, Miriam and Marcellina Cooney.

Illustrations: © Philip Hood, © Susan Hellard/ Arena. © Adrian Barclay, © Darrell Warner/ Beehive Illustration; © Catherine Ward, © Gilly Marklew/ S.G.A.

Permissions credits: Pages 7,10,11,17,28,29,44,63,86: © Lorenzo Lees. Page 19: The Annunciation by Dante Gabriel Rossetti (1828-82) Christie's Images, London, UK/Bridgeman Art Library, The Annunciation by Edward Reginald Frampton (1872-1923) Private Collection/Bridgeman Art Library. Page 20: The Annunciation, c.1438-45 (fresco) by Fra Angelico (Guido di Pietro) (c.1387-1455) Museo di San Marco dell'Angelico, Florence, Italy/Bridgeman Art Library. Page 21: (Detail) The Annunciation by Edward Reginald Frampton (1872-1923) Private Collection/Bridgeman Art Library. Page 24: The Vladimir Madonna of Humility, Russian icon (tempera on panel) by Simon Ushakov (1626-86) State Russian Museum, St. Petersburg, Russia/Bridgeman Art Library, © Leonard de Selva/CORBIS, The Virgin in Prayer, 1640-50 (oil on canvas) by Il Sassoferrato (Giovanni Battista Salvi) (1609-85) National Gallery, London, UK/Bridgeman Art Library, Madonna and Child, stained glass window designed by Roth Miksa (1865-1944) and Sandor Nagy (1868-1950) by Roth Miksa (1865-1944) Magyar Nemzeti Galeria, Budapest, Hungary/Bridgeman Art Library. Page 27: The Visitation by Philippe de Champaigne (1602-74) Noortman, Maastricht, Netherlands/Bridgeman Art Library. Pages 34,35,36 Misereor Lenten Veil by Almeyehu Bizuneh © Misereor Medienproduktion und Vertriebsgesellschaft mbh, Aachen, Germany. Page 41: Return of the Prodigal Son, c.1668-69 (oil on canvas) by Rembrandt Harmensz van Rijn (1606-69) Hermitage, St. Petersburg, Russia/Bridgeman Art Library. Page 56: The Last Supper by Leonardo da Vinci (1452-1519) Santa Maria delle Grazie, Milan, Italy/Bridgeman Art Library. Page 62: Collage © Bill Ross/CORBIS, © W. Cody/CORBIS, © Ed Young/CORBIS, © Gunter Marx/CORBIS. Page 64: © Bill Ross/CORBIS. Page 65: The Resurrection, c.1463 (fresco) by Piero della Francesca (c.1419/21-92) Pinacoteca, Sansepolcro, Italy/Bridgeman Art Library. Page 67: © Andes Press Agency/Carlos Reyes Manzo.